STEEL STALLIONS MC PREQUEL

HOSTILE ILLUSIONS

AWARD WINNING AUT

INDIA R. AD

STEEL STALLIONS MC PREQUEL

HOSTILE ILLUSIONS

AWARD WINNING AUTHOR

INDIA R. ADAMS

AUTHOR NOTE

Hostile Illusions was originally released in The Institute Anthology. Now that The Institute Anthology has come to an end, I am finally allowed to give readers what they have been asking for.

More!

I've received so many messages from readers, begging for more for these characters that
I had every intention on writing another book to add to this story, but my imagination likes to do its own thing; another character from the Haunted Roads series revealed a secret to me.
Hence, this re-release, in this manner.
Hostile Illusions now has an epilogue that may, well, you'll see.
Be sure to read on after that epilogue for incredible news and what's to come for these characters.

DEDICATION

To the ones who fell through the cracks
I stand with you
I am with you
I am one of you
#DamagedSoulsAreWorthSaving

PROLOGUE
Evermore...

Cruelty and all its power
Why am I the game of each hour?
Every pain, every slice...
It was not only me in this deadly vise

A s I lie here, life draining from my body, there is a clarity present that is bringing me cherished peace. I smile in relief, knowing that there is truly an Evermore...

The trees above me bow and bend to the wind that rushes through. A few leaves surrender to the grand force and fall from where they once belonged. I watch them float downward as if dancing in celebration for my choice.

I exhale... *Choice. It is finally mine.*

CHAPTER ONE
finding Vera

Parallel lives, side by side
Not knowing why I want to hide.
Murky shadows, distant memories
Will they ever become one?

How do you outrun something that doesn't exist? I see them. I feel their hatred toward me, yet I am told, over and over, they are merely illusions my mind has created.

With the ultimate kindness he always offers, my psychiatrist, Doctor Vincent Landon, asks, "Are they still behind me, Vera?"

Wondering what my true name is, I stare at the four faceless dark figures looming behind his chair. Their shoulders project a strength I'm eerily concerned can bring harm. I can't be positive, since I don't know who they are, but I sense their malice. Unfortunately, I don't even know who *I* am. Doctor Landon was gracious when giving me the name Vera so that I would have something to hold on to. And I am grateful. But, still, I feel so alone with no past to refer to.

With my arms hugging my bent legs to my chest, I sit in the soft, cushiony office chair that is supposed to help relax me. Nothing can calm my fear. It is all-consuming. There is no calm when I am always sensing danger lurking. My armpits are dripping with sweat, and it's hard to inhale. My lungs are constricted with terror. My bare toes keep trying to shelter one another, but there is nowhere for any part of me to hide.

I am exposed and feeling defenseless.

In his office, Doctor Landon sits across from me. He observes my thumb nervously rubbing along the impressive scar on my left forearm. Every time I use my left hand, I see it and get upset, not understanding why the scar unnerves me. Doctor Landon lets me wear long-sleeved shirts because of it. The slight curves at the bottom and top of the leathered skin almost make the defilement resemble an S, making me feel labeled. Just the thought has me shuddering...

"Are they saying anything to you?" asks Doctor Landon.

Attempting to hide my face against my covered knees, I whisper, "No." It's moments like this that I feel like a child, not the young woman I appear to be. Doctor Landon suspects I am approximately eighteen years old. I apprehensively add, "They're laughing."

With a needed calm, he asks, "Do you know why they are laughing?"

Pulling at my short, unevenly cut, blonde hair that I sense was once long, I start to rock, desperate for relief from the unknown panic threatening to knock me unconscious. It makes no sense. I don't even know who the shadowy figures are, yet they endlessly terrify me.

"Vera, you are doing so good. Try to remember—"

My spine straightens. "R-Remember?" He knows I hate to search for a memory that has epically failed me.

Doctor Landon exhales a steady breath as if buying time to determine his next approach. He does this often. "Yes. It is imperative that we learn how you arrived here."

My voice wobbles in fear, repeating what he already knows. "I walked."

The Serenity Institute has been my home for the past couple of months.

It's a very old building that reminds me of a castle that has been long forgotten in the countryside. The ceilings are tall, and the woodwork announces history and skillful craftsmanship. There is a grand, sweeping staircase that leads to the third floor where my room is located. Doctor Landon's office is on the first floor.

Police have been trying to learn my identity since I arrived here. I have no memory of where I came from. All I can recollect is stumbling through a forest, my clothes tattered, dirty, and bloodied.

Wounds. I had wounds everywhere.

That is how Doctor Landon found me. He had been walking to the institute's parking lot when he saw me tripping past the trees surrounding this facility.

I was lost, hungry, and beyond confused.

"Vera? Can you try and tell me what happened before we found you?" Doctor Landon sets his pad of paper on the little wooden antique end table that blends perfectly with the setting. He easily reaches with his long arms that balance his six-foot frame.

Daring to search my memory, although it is always with the same result, I feel my face wince as pain travels throughout my body. Sharp stabs of pain start in my thin left thigh and creep upward. Denying myself the sensation of feeling the raised, tough skin, my fingers don't touch the scar down the left side of my skinny neck either.

When I was found, I remember Doctor Landon yelling for help as he ran across the vast front property of Serenity. Two orderlies then came barreling out the front door, all showing signs of horror on their faces.

After having my physical wounds looked after in a medical hospital, a judge gave Doctor Sterling, the owner of Serenity Institute, temporary guardianship over me. Police stopped asking me questions once they believed my memory was nonexistent. Doctor Landon doesn't agree. He says I have hidden my past to protect myself.

My arms tighten around my legs as I shake my head, tears forming in my hazel eyes.

Doctor Landon leans forward, resting his elbows on his thighs that I doubt are scarred like mine. He softly assures me, "You're safe here. I won't let anyone hurt you."

I choke down tears, fear, and uncertainty plaguing me because I trust Doctor Landon, but he's wrong. The figures standing behind him are promising me agony. And I somehow know that no one can stop them.

Doctor Landon tries another tactic. "Vera, do you think you liked dolls when you were a little girl?" Even though my brows bunch, he continues. "I have a daughter. When she was much younger, she could sit on the floor for hours, combing her dolls' hair and dressing them in a variety of outfits. She would even pack them bags when we were traveling—" He stops when he sees me struggling to pull air into my lungs. "Does the word 'traveling' bother you?"

"I don't know." I rub the back of my neck as a searing pain takes over my mouth. My tongue searches the left side of my gums for the phantom ache, only to find the empty space that once held a molar.

Doctor Landon nods after studying my jaw move. "Yes, Vera. Ask questions about yourself." I don't. So, he does. "Why do you think only one molar is missing?" I stay quiet, still clueless. "Orthodontists usually remove more than one, especially when the other three are also in need." I stay silent. "Vera, that was a recent abstraction. Your mouth had yet to heal when I found you."

"Maybe... I did it? Maybe I ate something that hurt me?"

He huffs. "Do you know how hard it is to remove a tooth like that? Especially on yourself?" The shadows behind him start to stir, causing me to gasp, and my heart pounds wildly. "No," gently reminds my psychiatrist. "Don't let them stop you. Try to see only me, Vera."

Swallowing hard due to intense nerves and the sensation of not being able to breathe properly, I pull my eyes away from the threat. "They-They—"

He leans forward. "They what? Say it. You can do this."

I huddle into my legs again, then whisper, "They scare me."

I don't see it but can hear his slight smile. It always changes the sound of his mature voice. "It's okay to be scared." His antique chair creaks as he leans back. "Do you know why they scare you?" My rapid exhales blow across my sweatpants and beat against my clammy cheeks. "Do you think they had anything to do with the old scars on the left side of your body?" When I refuse to answer, he almost whispers, "I'm so proud of you."

This is the first time I haven't run from his office and back upstairs to my room. The shadows usually win. His pride in me is the only thing keeping me rooted to this chair. He cares. I need him to. It gives me comfort I don't want to lose.

My strained voice cracks. "You never give up on me." We've had so many "talks" that seem futile, without any progression, in my opinion, but Doctor Landon is always pleased at the end of each session.

"How could I?" Without looking, I hear his smile is full now. "You are one of the most special people I have *ever* met. You have come so far because you are so brave."

I don't understand why he says these things, but those words and his honesty give me the courage to come out of hiding. Only one other person makes me feel like I may be safe someday. He is much younger than Doctor Landon but just as important. Continuing to gaze at my doctor, my forehead refusing to leave my knees, I try to understand why the shadows scare me.

As if reading me and seeing my silent decision to dare and poke into my past, Doctor Landon doesn't move or speak. Slowly, I close my eyes, searching for an inkling of my lost life, and try to picture a little girl playing with dolls...

In pitch black, I'm on my side, folded into a ball that is so tightly confined I can barely breathe. My cheeks are wet as I cry, wanting to be set free. "Pwease? Pwease, let me out."

"Oh, God. I'm a little girl." My eyes don't open due to being lost in this memory that promises to be horrid, but my heart demands I tell my doctor what I'm witnessing. It is uncanny to see this from my older self's point of view, yet be living it at the same time.

A tiny bit of relief from the growing fear takes place when Doctor Landon can barely contain his eagerness. "How old, Vera? Try to remember."

A hand touches the material holding me captive. "Packed tight," announces a male voice.

Overwhelmed with being in two worlds at once, I cry, "He sounds a little older than me." I can't help but rub my forearm, wanting to erase my scar.

"Who, Vera? Do you know him?"

"Is the zipper locked?"

Almost moaning due to the terror, I tell him, "So does he."

Doctor Landon sounds concerned. "There is more than one?"

Metal quietly clanks, then there's a tug on my entrapment. "Yeah. It's locked."

It's getting even harder to breathe, but I force out, "And his."

"Th-Three?" asks my stunned doctor.

A disturbing excitement laces the next voice. "Let's drag her to the top of the stairs."

Dread. I'm instantly consumed with dread. "Four." Even though I am trapped in a memory, I'm not clueless about its possible connection to the four shadows that haunt the older me.

Doctor Landon is speaking to me, but I can no longer comprehend what he's saying. I'm too horrified that the shadows have a much deeper meaning and are connected with what's about to happen to me—or what already happened to me.

The bag I'm in makes a swish sound as it's dragged across hard flooring. It's drowning out the crying... The bag is so thin, I can feel the coldness from the floor. I want the little girl to scream for help, but I sense she—I—know it will do us no good.

"You ready?" This one sounds as if he's about to step onto a roller-coaster ride he has waited for all his young years.

Four sets of hands are placed on me. My heart cracks, feeling how I'm almost too small to give them all space to touch me. My heart cracks because not one of these boys is mentioning how cruel this is or how they shouldn't do it. No. The four of them are in a pack—an agreement. I don't know who they are or why I am with them, and I have no time to figure it out.

The four sets of hands, after a celebrated count to three, push, sending me on a spiral that's only the beginning of my downfall.

CHAPTER TWO
Loving Tate

After falling, I find it hard to stand
So, I carefully turn to a helping hand.
After remembering, I find it impossible to be blind.
With his love, I hope to never be left behind.

Lying in the dark, what I'm seeing is making my red—exhausted from crying—eyes heal. The moonlight glows on Tate as he opens the window to my bedroom at Serenity. His smile is the softness I need in this unkind world.

"Hi," he whispers so that no patients, doctors, or orderlies hear him.

Seventeen. What an age to be. Tate is not quite a man, yet he yearns to be one. A cub striving to be a lion so he can lead, guard, and nurture. Not all wisdom is his yet, but he gazes at me as if I'm the only star in his night.

The first time he came to me here at Serenity, I was somewhat alarmed, watching him run across the grass from the woods. No one saw him but me. I was in the garden of flowers with Doctor Landon. The sun had been bright and warming to a lost soul. I was in a state of unusual ease when Doctor Landon was pulled away by an orderly who had a question.

As soon as Tate ran up to the electric fence, being careful not to touch it, any apprehension I had dissipated. Something in his blue eyes, which reminded me of a deep river, felt like the closest to a home that I may have ever had. From under his shaggy, dark blond hair, he was out of breath but smiling. He whispered, "I couldn't help but notice how beautiful you are."

Seeing his raw innocence was a breath of fresh air. "Who are you?" I whispered to not gain my doctor or orderly's attention.

Precious dimples deepened. "Willing to find out?" The sun's rays on his soft skin dared me to deny the delivered gift.

That day, Tate brought on my first desire to smile since arriving at Serenity. Until Tate, I'm not sure if I ever smiled before. His visits have been my only happiness.

Now, here he is again, the sight of him bringing me an amazing solace.

I wipe a remaining tear before it hits my pillow and quietly say, "Hi."

Crawling through the open window, he keeps smiling with a bravery that would calm the spirit of any lost young woman. "Nah, pretty girl. Nah." He stands tall after shutting the window. "No cryin' tonight." He brushes long, wavy, dark blond bangs from his adorable face while he walks toward me. "Only sugar."

A relieved chuckle escapes me because I know what he means. And I want it.

His face lights up with joy that shouldn't belong to such youth. From what I understand, teenage boys are rough and always causing mischief. Not Tate. He only creates joy. "Oh. I see you like my kisses."

I do. He tastes as sweet as his heart is.

Mine sighs, knowing it can rest now that this young man has come for the night.

Tate pulls back my blanket and sheet. Warmth rolls through my body and soul as his hand tenderly pushes on my shoulder to roll me to my back, then he rests his body on top of mine. "Is there anyone else who can give you sugar like me?"

My arms demand to hold him again, so I indulge. Nothing feels like Tate does. He is wholesome. He is pure. He is... hope.

Until tonight with Doctor Landon, I never understood why I treasured Tate as much as I have over the last couple of months. Now that I'm learning I may have a traumatic past, I can't help but wonder if I recognize Tate to be a light in my life. One that I must cling to in order to survive the darkness in my lonely mind.

Staring up at this incredible person, I whisper, "I finally had a memory tonight."

His smile fades.

A sting jabs my heart. "You don't seem happy for me."

Sorrow vibrates from his expression of remorse. "I can't. All those memories once brought you pain. I had hoped—" He sighs in some sort of regret. "I had actually hoped they wouldn't come back." His eyes look so sad. "It must be *me* bringing them back."

This is the first time Tate has spoken of my past as if familiar with it. "Did you know me before I came here?"

I stare at him, hungry for answers, but he doesn't indulge me. He only stares at the window for a moment as if contemplating on something. Then, as if finally making a decision, he studies his hand while lifting it to hover over me and waits. My head tilts. Not because I don't know what he is waiting for, but because I *do*. Somehow, I comprehend his request and slowly lift my palm until it meets his.

Our eyes meet before his fingers gradually slide between mine. He whispers with so much affection, "Hold my heart, Pretty Girl."

Emotions bloom in my chest. My fingers fold down to hold his hand, his heart, and offer mine. "Evermore."

A slight smile, full of so much more then I seem to be able to comprehend, returns to his gorgeous face. "And there is our promise."

After a powerful moment that lingers between us as if infusing our souls, affectionate lips touch mine, soothing away the rest of the pain my memories have brought me.

Being young and enthralled with each other, many kisses have transpired, but tonight is different. It's as if my newfound memories have changed everything. Soon, our mouths no longer meet with a bashful yet elated manner how we usually kiss. Now, I feel the kiss growing into a sincere and fulfilling passion. Licks of our tongues call out for more touches. We are no longer timid with each other as our cravings overpower any limits we believed existed.

As he kisses my neck, my heart pounds, and my belly tingles with needs that cause a pulsing between my thighs. With no reservations, I open them, inviting Tate to slip between my legs. As his body sinks, his clothed, hardened length meets my core. He groans his pleasure, and his mouth widens to possess mine, again and again. Gasping for air, I meet his desperation with my own, driven by our ravaged kissing union.

Soon, Tate's body shakes with an innocent starvation. It's almost as if he doesn't understand what his body needs. He seems surprised when his hips move against me, searching for delicious friction. We both moan with relief as his erection punishes my groin. But that satisfaction is short-lived because our bodies are now in an even more heightened state.

My panties are damp. I want Tate to take us past where we've been.

As if hearing my call, his actions become bolded. His innocent needs grow into a man's appetite in only minutes. He palms my breast with tender squeezes as if his hand has a mind of its own, wanting to know every curve. I groan, and my hips tilt upward when his thumb swipes past my nipple. Understanding I liked it, he touches it again, his famished kiss deepening at the same time.

Under him, I feel sheltered and protected. He owns all that he can reach of me. I can't help but love the sensation to the point I desire for him to touch even more.

With lust, Tate stares at me as I slide my hands under his shirt to feel his warm skin. His wet lips are spread in wonder as I pull on his back, wanting him closer, even though it is not possible with clothes on. I plead, "Please, don't say no," for all he can give this lost girl. I crave a deeper connection with him. I crave feeling grounded and with a purpose. Since Tate is all I have, I want all of him.

His meaningful eyes never leave mine as he balances on his knees to remove his shirt. "I could never say no, but—"

When he stalls, insecurities rise, but I don't let them win. I want this. My bare inner thighs timidly rub against his jeans, hoping to spur him to proceed. "Tate, take these off."

Apparently, his hormones are no match for his conscience or my lack of self-control. I giggle when Tate hops out of the bed and frantically strips as if scared I may change my mind. I hold back a gasp when his erection pops free. Maybe the surprise is because I might not have ever seen one before. Maybe I've seen a hundred, but I know at this very second, Tate's will be the only one I will remember. That makes my soul soar with a freedom amnesia can't touch.

Grinning like a guilty cake thief, Tate crawls back between my legs. "You find my torture funny?" He sits on his feet, his thick thighs no longer reminding me of a young man. Tate has been hiding a full-grown body under baggier clothes.

"Torture?" I playfully snicker.

He licks at lips that appear famished. "Yeah. I want you so bad it hurts."

Since my ego is inflated properly, I respond with, "Then why am I still in this?" I lay my arms over my head and pillow to hint at the removal of my clothes.

Tate lifts a brow, accepting my challenge, but after he starts lifting the hem of my sweatshirt, his naked chest pants and his eyes are no longer focused on mine. There is no bra to hide my breasts. I am exposed... "Umm, Tate?"

"Oh shit. Sorry."

Halfway through undressing me, Tate gets distracted, leaving my oversized sweatshirt covering my face and my arms trapped above my head.

Tate yanks it off me, trying to muffle a laugh. "Damn, I got so distracted with the best set of boobs in the whole world."

"Whole world?" I dip my chin. "You are forgiven." I've lost him again. "Tate?"

He wipes at his mouth as if expecting to feel drool. "You're only wearing these."

Tate gestures to my white cotton panties. I almost purr, "I don't want to be."

As if trying to have some self-control, his hands tremble while he reaches forward and pulls down my underwear. I don't cover myself with a hand or blanket. I let him gander at all I want to give him. The cool evening air finds my heat, exciting me further.

Breathlessly, Tate tells me, "I've never seen anything so beautiful."

I tease, "Not even my face?"

With worry, his eyes snap to mine until he sees I'm only kidding. Dimples appear, complimenting his smirk. "What's between your legs is no comparison to that face. Your hazel eyes are my undoing. I swear it. And your long golden hair? Don't get me started."

Something pokes at my mind. *But my hair is short—*

"Jesus, Pretty Girl. You, naked, is killing me. Look at this," he heavily whispers while pointing to his erection that is possibly possessing all the blood in his body.

"Can I?" I expose my palm, gesturing to his manhood.

Tate swallows and nods as if I have offered him the world. "Y-Yeah. Sure. I—I'm totally okay with dat—I mean th-at." With a nervous and excited hand, I reach forward and grip his erection. Still on his knees, his eyes drift shut and his head falls back. "Your hand feels *so* much better than mine."

Muffling a giggle, I stroke his shaft. "Just what every girl dreams of hearing."

As my hand pulls on his sensitive skin, Tate moans, "Oh, God," before melting forward. Balancing on his knees, he catches himself with one hand and hovers over me. I don't release him. He seems lost in me stroking him. His free hand has a vice grip on my hip. There are raised veins in his neck and forehead. "Please, don't stop what you're doing, but I'm desperate to know what *you* feel like."

My chest starts panting again, elated about feeling him touching me down there. My voice sounds weak and shaky. "Okay."

I'm so focused on his movements; it's challenging to keep my hand stroking him. Tate's hand slides from my hip, across my lower belly, and down over my pubic bone.

Even though his mouth doesn't always seem to be moving, I can still hear him speak. It's like I can read his mind—his thoughts.

As his fingers softly sink down and between my folds, Tate hisses, "So wet... Why is you being so wet making my mouth water?" He doesn't wait for a response. With his one hand, he pushes off the mattress to sit back on his feet to get a full view of me. He doesn't even mention the fact that he's pulled his erection free of my hand. He seems too entranced to notice. "I can't believe I've been missing out on this my whole life." His fingers rub up and down my core.

My hands grip the fitted sheet underneath me as I groan. "Tate." His warm fingertips are compounding the sensation of cold air and bringing me such pleasure I think I'm seeing stars.

A middle finger searches my opening. "Can... Can I—"

"Yes. Please, yes."

The finger glides into me so perfectly, as if it's meant to be there.

Tate keeps closing his mouth to swallow as if I'm truly making his mouth water. Then he reopens it to breathe as if there is no other possible way to inhale. I think he loves every minute of this. Tate seems only able to see my juncture while his finger slides in and out of me. "You're so soft." His thumb rubs over my clit, causing me to arch, bearing down on his hand. His breathing is erotically erratic. "Tell me if you want me to stop."

My head flails side to side. "Don't you dare."

Another finger joins the delicious torture, his thumb not slowing. There is no pain or discomfort at all. It dawns on me that I'm most likely not a virgin. The only shame in the matter is that someone may have been here before Tate.

Never again.

In delightful abandon, my legs fall open.

My feet spread. I want Tate to have full access to claim what will always be his.

Air is rushing in and out of his gaping mouth. "I've never been so turned on in my life."

His fingers delve deeper, sending me into a frenzy. A sensational build has my core throbbing with heat and absolute need. I need to stay quiet, but it's becoming impossible. "T-Tate, I'm... I... Go harder."

Tate rushes back to hover over me, one hand bracing him while his other works my channel like an instrument, ringing noises out of me as I beg for the release his efforts are promising. His mouth slams to mine, muffling my cry as an orgasm rips through me with such a force it feels like a savage beast just mystically staked a claim over my whole body.

Forehead to forehead, our gasping mixes together like two storms joining forces.

His hand finally slips from my exasperated core and grips the nape of my neck. I can feel my wetness on his fingers, smearing against my skin as if Tate is reminding me what he just did to me. He owned my body. But it is not domination that his words speak of. It is adoration.

"I love you."

I have no way of knowing if those words have ever been spoken to me before, but I'm thankful. I only want to hear them from Tate. "Be with me."

His sharp inhale tells me Tate knows exactly what I mean. Bracing his weight on his hands that are on each side of my head, his biceps shake, but not from a lack of strength. I think he is fighting for patience. Cautiously, and without breaking eye contact with me, Tate lowers his body. His elbows sink to the mattress, and his legs unfold. We keep staring at each other, both anticipating the touch so new to us. We both gasp at the slight contact. He swallows again when my pelvis tilts, asking for his entry.

Tate slips his hands under my shoulders and grips them tightly. "Evermore," he whispers before his arm muscles contract, pulling his body forward.

We both take a quick inhale when the tip of his penis enters me. The sensation of a body joining mine is bewildering and fulfilling beyond the physical feeling. It feels as if our two souls are blending. As he surges, every stretch of my inner wall is welcomed. I become his, and he becomes mine. It's a wonderful awareness since it's possible I've never belonged to anyone.

Once he fills me, pelvis to pelvis, my body melts into the bed. I want to yell "yes" because I'm in Heaven, but don't want anyone to learn he's in here with me. That would mean an end to this beautiful, much-needed night. So, in silence, I rock with the young man moving above me like a soft melody to my restless spirit. Gentle thrusts are the music we dance to. Sweat is our only blanket, and it's wonderful.

As if being the one needing to be silenced this time, Tate places his open lips to mine. Greedy moans echo in my mouth as his body shudders its own orgasm. The thought that a part of him is floating inside my channel makes me hope we never stop making love tonight. Ambitious, my hands tightly grip his butt and pull him deeper, begging his movements not to end.

Barely able to breathe, his tongue dives in my mouth as if he may eat me alive from the inside out. I don't care. In fact, I welcome the attack as long as he keeps bringing me this immense pleasure that is radiating through everything that I am.

Buttocks flex and retract under my hands, his shaft delving and gliding in both our fluids. Tate surrenders to his climax yet has no hesitation in attempting to build another. This time, I feel a stir so deep in my core, my fingers dig into his muscles—the only action I can take to not wake anyone through my second orgasm.

As my body reaps the reward of such a high, Tate surges toward another climax. His head falls to my neck as his hands tighten, pulling on my shoulders so he can sink deeper inside of me. He holds his breath as the next ejaculation rips through his inexperienced body.

When he finally catches his breath, he slowly pulls his face to mine. His eyes widen when he sees my tears. But I smile. "Only happy ones."

A smile grows across his sweaty face, too. "Yes, only happy ones... Lacey."

Gasp.

CHAPTER THREE
Disciplined 'ain

Will I ever find peace? Or forever be on my knees?
There is no rhyme, no reason, for all this unknown treason
Memories must be found
Or I shall never be sound

"You are very quiet today," notices my doctor as we sit in Serenity's flower garden. I appreciate the thoughtfulness behind such a serene place for the patients, and my doctor's kindness for suggesting we be outdoors. But the sun is hiding behind some clouds, not helping my dreary mood. The quiet is much cherished, though. I have a lot on my mind.

Sitting across the table from Doctor Landon, I stare at the dark figures looming behind him. "I'm not sure what to trust." I had a beautiful evening with Tate last night and was feeling so much better, but I must've fallen asleep. He was gone when I woke. I never had the chance to ask why he called me Lacey, nor did I get to say goodbye after such a monumental evening. This is leaving me feeling overwhelmed and nervous.

Doctor Landon studies my eyes and how they are not focused on him. Only beyond... "Just because you see illusions doesn't mean you are delusional."

Forcing myself to look away, I take a sip of water from a plastic cup. Glass is not an option. Patients could break it and permanently escape our unwanted reality. I've already explained to Doctor Landon I would never take my own life, but I haven't told him why. If he knew of the boy sneaking through my window, I'm sure he would disapprove. Tate's visits are my only peace. "Your claim is a bit confusing."

He sits back in his chair. Stray sunrays appear and shine off his greying hair. "Just because you are seeing... *things* that I may not see doesn't mean it's not happening. What if the four men behind me are real? Not at this moment, of course, but elsewhere."

A chill seizes my breath to the point my hand races to my chest to beg my heart to keep beating. I dare a peek at the figures behind him.

He folds his hands in his lap. "I don't think you have a Delusional Disorder. I fear—" He catches himself. "I *believe* what you see behind me are memories. You have Dissociative Amnesia. I believe your memories are fighting to come forward. Maybe for good reason."

Even with the sip of water, my lips are dry again. "So, I can get better?" I sound desperate, I know, but I am. I want this—whatever my life is—to be over.

"Or," he pauses as if debating on how much to say but finally relinquishes, "protect yourself," then studies me.

His meaning dawns on me, but possibly not how he would expect. "Do you think those... people... would want to hurt someone I know? Or care for?" *Would they hurt Tate? Should I tell Doctor Landon so he can help protect him?*

Doctor Landon smiles. "That is so kind of you, Vera, but I will remain safe, I assure you."

Nervously, I nod, understanding why he assumed I was speaking of him. Doctor Landon believes he's the only person I know. I gasp when a realization hits me.

"What is it, Vera?"

I stare at the shadows behind Doctor Landon, wondering why they haven't appeared behind Tate whenever he visits. "Why are they always behind *you?*" Agitated, I gesture about. "There are other patients here. Other doctors I see with them. A-And orderlies." My skin breaks out into a sweat. "Why only you?"

"Truth? No holding back?"

My nostrils flare at his ridiculous question.

He surrenders as if stepping outside of his normal doctor mode. "I happen to believe it's because your subconscious knows I can help you remember." He winces while shaking his head. "I don't think you want to." He mumbles, "Most likely, rightfully so." Then he shrugs, possibly wanting to relax my growing tension. "Or, it can be as simple as you never converse with anyone other than me."

I look away because that is not exactly accurate.

"Vera? Have you spoken to anyone other than me?"

Panicking to change the subject, I blurt, "I think my name may be Lacey."

My doctor sits up straight and stutters in shock and glee. "W-What? Really? Did you have another memory?"

Dismissively, I shrug, happy he is no longer inquiring about Tate. "Just heard that name in my head."

He exhales as if utterly pleased with this breakthrough that is rocking my lonely world. "This is incredible, Ver—" Doctor Landon sighs, "Lacey."

Not sure why, I suddenly feel completely annoyed. My jaw is rigid, and I want to hit something. I almost growl, "Can I go to my room now?"

Doctor Landon blinks in dismay before finding his professional attitude. "Will you first explain why you seem so frustrated all of a sudden?"

I stand so fast my chair slides back in a rush. "You're the doctor! You tell me!" My sudden rage is bewildering and uncontrollable, but I can't help but think of what Tate told me; *"All those memories once brought you pain."* So, I spew, "Maybe it's because this news may be awful. Who *is* Lacey? What is she like? Does she even want to be found?" I start to angry cry. "Does she *want* to be lost?" I walk around my chair and stand behind it, resting my tense hands on the back of it. "Am I even her?" I rattle the chair. *"Why are you smiling at me?"*

"You're asking questions!" Happily, he stands. "Look at you!" He heavily whispers with emotions, "You're *fighting* for your future. You actually *want* to know more."

After I pause to consider his meaning, my knees give, so I hold on to the back of the chair and squat while trying to catch my breath. I let my head hang because I unexpectedly feel it is too weighted to lift. I'm not sure how many moments have passed before I ask, "What if my future is bleak?"

Doctor Landon kneels at my side and sounds hopeful. "What if it is full of joy? What if, by not fighting for what's yours, you miss out on bliss?"

Tate... I rub at my chest. I simply cannot handle the thought of being without him. But then I remember the dark figures may want to hurt him. "Will you think bad of me if I tell you I'm still scared?"

Doctor Landon chuckles. "Not all. I can only be impressed that you are so brave to admit what anyone would be feeling right now in your shoes."

Tears drip from my eyes and onto the pavers under my feet. "Doctor Landon?"

"Yes," his smile grows as he attempts to temporarily name me, "Whoever You Choose To Be."

Choice... That word and what it entails somehow erupts inside me. I burst into tears, so desperate to have such power and authority over my own life. The war of emotions in my heart is screaming that this so-called human right has never been mine. This all makes no sense and is confusing me further.

Needing affection on such a sincere level, I start to lean into my doctor but stop myself.

Doctor Landon is a smart man and reads my actions. I sigh when his arms pull me to him. "I'm here for you. As long as you need me to be."

Again, simple words spoken rock through my soul as if they are words I have desperately yearned to hear, yet never have. "Thank you," I cry. "Even if you're are the only person who has never given up on me, I promise to never forget you."

His embrace tightens. "That is an honor coming from someone with amnesia." His head rests on top of mine in a fatherly manner that pokes at me somewhere deep inside.

Even after returning to my room, I keep feeling an invisible nudge to my gut, like a bubble from far below the surface of an ocean, racing toward freedom, the surface silently promises. The bubble wants to burst into the night air and transform into a breeze it has always dreamt of being. Yes, I decide, I want to be where I belong. I want to *know*!

Pacing in my dark room with only one lamp lit, I think of how Doctor Landon held me. How it felt fatherly. And safe. *Do I have a father? Is he looking for me?*

I start banging on my chest that now feels as if something is missing. Or *someone* is missing—

Pain suddenly sears through my soul as if God himself has let loose his fury. But what does this pain mean? *What is it that I'm not remembering?* Letting my tired head fall back, I beg to the Heavens above, "What do you want me to know?"

Answered prayers are not always beautiful.

At first, fragments of memories pelt my mind and gut in a disorienting manner that has my stomach souring. Emotions, both alarming and disheartening, flood my newfound muddled state. I see places, faces, smiles, and disturbing grimaces, all making me experience a mental earthquake of sorts.

Then, a memory slams into me as if I have been shoved into an old movie house and forced to watch the cinematic event from the actor's point of view.

Just like that, I remember my home, my family... and all I fear about some of them...

Around the age of six, in my parents' garage, I laid on a wooden workshop table, not by my own free will. My two older brothers were present—ten-year-old twins, Jarod and Jake. They had brown eyes and short dark hair like my father's. I was more of my mother. She had blonde hair and green eyes.

The other two boys present were the twins' best friends, Damien and Crow. Damien, with haunting blue eyes, was eleven. Crow, also with spooky blue eyes, was ten. Both had blondish hair that laid flat.

Jake and Crow were holding down my upper body by force. It was easy for them with me so small and defenseless. Their young faces were evilly elated with my struggles. Their breathing matched my panicked breaths but for much different reasons. Pain was creating mine. Pleasure created theirs.

Jarod was holding down my legs. I cried, "What's happening?" when I felt Damien touch cold metal to the bottom of my feet. I got no spoken responses, but curious eyes studied me as hands unexpectedly lifted, releasing me. I quickly tried to sit up and escape, but my whole little body suddenly seized, contorting with no muscle control while electric shocks shot through me.

My crippled body collapsed back to the table when the electrocution ended. Laughter erupted instead of pity.

Jarod cheered, "Did you see that?"

Crow smiled in amazement, then demanded, "Do it again!"

Without a chance to catch my breath, my tiny body arched off the wooden table, only the back of my head and heels supporting me. With my jaw locked, I painfully felt frozen in time before crashing back into reality. My back slammed to the wood beneath me when the electric zap ended again. There were no tender touches checking on my wellbeing.

Only mad curiosity.

I'm not sure how many times I was electrocuted by my brothers and their best friends before my head fell to the side in exhaustion and a shock not related to the electricity. My spirit seemed to take the heaviest jolt of all. My heart broke as my older brothers, figures who should have wanted to protect me, celebrated my anguish. Laughter mixed with high-fives and intense embraces as if these boys had unlocked the secret of life. They seemed enthralled with my mental terror as much as my physical affliction.

My torture feeds their needs.

My suffering is their natural high.

My misery is the outlet for their sadistic ways.

My despair... Their ecstasy.

A finger inquisitively swiped at the side of my mouth, somewhat pulling me from my daze. Jake stared at his finger as if witnessing a miracle. "She bit her tongue."

Four sets of eyes stared at the redness on his skin as if the sight beckoned them to become vampires. Hunger stirred within them all as their eyes refocused on me. Mouths *were gaping, sucking in air and exhaling in an aggressive manner. I felt as if they were preparing to tear into my flesh, savagely.*

So engrossed in their appalling high, the boys didn't hear my father come home or enter the garage, searching for his children. What he saw had him paling before screaming, "What the hell is this?" Daddy shoved the four boys out of the way, horrified. "What are you doing?" His eyes caught something near my feet. "Are you shocking her?"

An internal sigh exuded from me when hearing my rescuer arrive. There is a strength in good fathers that little girls look to for protection. That's why I had told him about my brothers being mean to me. But Daddy had said, "Boys will be boys. Don't tell Mama. It will only make her worry. I'll have a talk with the boys."

I don't know if this talk ever took place, but now Daddy was yelling, "Is this what she meant by you 'hurting' her?"

Now, looking back, I recognize the unexpected pleasure all four torturers were experiencing when getting caught. My father's horror seemed to be as pleasurable to them as was my pain. My young heart was grateful for the man who had come to save me, unaware of what was truly happening.

After noticing who was with my brothers, Daddy's lips twisted in disgust. "And you two? I will be telling your parents..."

Shaken from the trauma, I couldn't sit up on my own, so my dad helped me, holding me to him. My ear rested on his chest, hearing his stampeding heart and yells of fury. My stunned feet dangled off a side of the table. The rest of me felt like I no longer possessed bones. Even though my thoughts were hazy, my adrenaline had given me the clarity to notice Jarod ignoring Dad's ranting and pulling a bottle of something from a shelf. Even at this young age, I was not as innocent as I should have been. Instead, I was becoming rapidly aware of the malice these brothers, together, could conjure. I touched Daddy's arm to make him alert of the lingering danger, but he was far too distraught to hear my silent warnings. All he saw was a recent burn on my palm. Realization blinded him. "Oh, God... Did they do this to you, too?" He screamed at the brothers, "You said she grabbed a hot spoon!"

Since I was only a child, every bruise I had made sense and caused no concern. Who would have imagined the truth? But, as I had learned the day the brothers burned me with a heated spoon, the boys' cravings were deepening. The electrocution was only a precursor of what else was to be inflicted on me.

As my dad continued to roar, "What the fuck is wrong with you kids?" finally understanding my wounds were not of my own doing, Jarod poured a bottle of motor oil on the floor. Right behind my dad.

My heart raced. I tried to open my mouth, but I was in some sort of shock. Not a word could pass my lips.

Like a well-trained pack of wolves, the four evil boys flanked my father from a slight distance, two on each side, and stalked forward. One, or even all four, were not enough to take my father down, so they got creative. They closed in to cause Daddy concern.

In disbelief at the aggression, my father yanked me from the table. My partially limp body hung from his chest and embrace, and he took a couple of steps backward. It didn't take long for the trap to work. A heavy foot flew out from under my dad, and he fell back, hitting his head on the concrete floor with a gruesome thud. I didn't have to see to understand what damage had been done. The final exhale from the chest I was laying on, and the arms releasing me to lifelessly fall to the wet ground, told me everything. Daddy was gone.

I couldn't move. Absolute disbelief had me frozen in place, on top of a dead body that once was dear to a little girl. Daddies are heroes. They are formidable. Nothing can hurt them. Mine, now dead, made the brothers the most dangerous beings on earth.

Sure not to step in the pool of oil, the boys slowly grouped together to see my unresponsive expression. Implausibly, they seemed disappointed to not get more of a reaction from me. I heard, "Why isn't she screaming?"

I couldn't even move as Damien squatted into my line of sight. Sinister blue eyes glared. "Want the same for your mom?"

My mother's smile, innocent of the madness, ignited in my fragile mind. The horror of something grave happening to her must have been noticeable in my eyes. Surrounding breaths sped up as they fed on my terror.

I looked to Jarod, but he was smiling, not reacting like a son who had just lost a father. A tear slipped from me and dripped to my Daddy's now quiet chest. I would mourn him, alone.

"Good," answered Damien before he stood and said, "Crow and I will go home. We weren't here. Got it? Crow and I will do the same for you after we take *my dad down." Then he instructed my brothers on how to react during the upcoming 911 phone call they were to make. They all schemed the perfect responses for the officers and any witnesses, my brothers crying over Daddy's "accident."*

I didn't continue to cry. I didn't move. I just watched as Daddy's blood mixed with the dark oil. A misfortunate lesson was concreted that day. Speak... and die.

I collapse to the bed in horror. Memories are now flooding my mind like a wave with no moon, giving gravity to the water. No fear can withhold the truth this time.

After Daddy's death, a cycle began. The four boys seemed to be chasing a first high like a Meth addict. My mother was too sad and under pressure to notice. She was now the sole provider, working two jobs and still financially struggling. My reclusive behavior was blamed on the tragic loss of a father figure.

Years began to pass from one tormented moment to the next. I was always in survival mode. I went to school and kept my grades up so as not to draw any attention to myself. I was quiet to the point that most never even noticed me. Teachers always called on the loud kids in my class.

I was left in a life of solitude, even when surrounded by others.

As I got older, so did my sadists. As their bodies started to have sexual cravings, these longings mixed with their sadistic behaviors. This made my early teenage years horrendous. I was instructed to hide all marks from my mother, her safety becoming the only thing I felt I had control over. I offered my body to protect hers.

After seeing my blood drip from my mouth the night my dad was killed, knives had become a favored type of torture. Starting with little cuts, they grew into something much more sinister. The unnatural brotherhood had done research on their evil desires and learned they were truly sadists at heart. Instead of being ashamed of this vile fact, they celebrated. I was a labeled conquest by yet another scar. To not be easily recognized as the letter S, representing sadism, the symbol was cut in a stretched manner down my forearm so I would never forget who I secretly belonged to.

Long sleeves became my best friend.

The shirts for warmth actually helped me ignore my rotten predicament.

At the boys' ages of fifteen and sixteen, erections would occur as my skin was being damaged. Their puberty had been in full swing long before their sexual interests in me, but they had girlfriends to satisfy simpler sensual cravings. That eventually changed.

Normal sexual relationships soon didn't suffice.

One night, Damien rubbed his clothed crotch while Jake sliced my inner thigh. I was in shorts, on my bathroom floor. They never cut me on carpet, not after making that mistake a few years prior. My mother had asked questions about the stain. I reminded her of my fictional clumsiness, saving her life once again.

When Jarod noticed the groping, he laughed. "What the fuck are you doing?"

"Sorry, dude. Kimberly is out of town, so I have no one to fuck while thinking of these cuts." He gestured to me as if I were a nuisance. "Look. We don't even have to hold her down anymore. She's getting boring."

Becoming so accustomed to the abuse, I had learned to discipline my pain. A simple cut was nothing anymore. I didn't cry or struggle, just laid there and let them slice away.

Jake, still with a blade in his hand, snarled at me. "He's right, you fucking boring whore."

"Whore," Jarod said to himself before glancing over his shoulder. "I bet you raping her will get a rile out of her."

My gasp was all they needed. The hungry wolves came back to life in that mere second. Like vultures to a carcass, they dove in. Except, I wasn't a dead, leftover piece of meat. I was alive and wanted to stay intact, not be ripped apart. So, I fought. Even though it fed my attackers, I battled with all I had. Hands grabbed at me, so I bit and hit and screamed as I was dragged out of the bathroom by my ankles. I swung madly as clothes were ripped from my body. The carpet burned my skin as I jerked and struggled to get free from the insane ones threatening to overtake me.

I was no match to the still-growing young men, but I was proud of not going down without being heard and felt. A few teeth marks, punches, and kicks landed before I was finally restrained.

Jarod instructed, "Condom up. I don't want her pregnant," as Damien removed his clothing in an eager hurry.

I, a female, was their ideal victim.
My fear, my pain, was their fuel.
I was terrified.
I fed them much.

The physical rape was only by one that night, but the mental rape was by them all. Sobbing in pain and heartbreak, I had to bear witness to more of my vital fluids bringing them joy. Virginal blood leaked from within me. The sacred liquid was touched and stolen by the onlookers. My two brothers and Crow reached between my legs after my spent rapist fell to the side, panting due to his elated state.

In shock, like I had felt on the night my father was murdered, I laid there, motionless. Used, body and soul, unaware my menstrual cycle would now become a special treat for my abusers. They felt they got to witness my stolen virginity on a monthly basis. I would be raped then tampered with as if only an object for their entertainment.

Soon, just like the cuts, the rapes lost their effect on me. The emotional shutdown took time since my own brothers joining in my terror was so unforgiving for me. They had done countless horrendous acts against me, but their sexual assaults were the most damaging to my mental health. Eventually, that shock was also something I learned to numb out.

When the terrorists' boredom set in again, due to my lack of "proper" reactions, the sadistic beings became inventive. They had to find something my body needed and would demand, no matter how much I tried to block out their atrocious crimes.

Air became their weapon.

CHAPTER FOUR
Sugar and Kisses

They weren't illusions at all.
They were memories.
Maybe that is the case for all of us.
We're not mad. We're simply... destroyed.

"**W**ake up, Lacey," cooed one of my assailants. "There's more fun to have." On my bedroom floor, my eyes fluttered open to report to my brain what predicament I was waking to. I had just passed out due to a plastic bag over my head. It was beyond terrifying. It was against nature. Not being able to breathe is against the one rule all humans must follow.

My foggy eyes widened in terror because I could see and feel that I was being held down on my bedroom floor, while Damien, now naked, climbed on top of my face. With a bent leg on each side of my head, he put his weight over my mouth to smother me with his testicles.

I had no control over my exertions, nor did I have control over the rest of the brothers holding me down until I slipped into unconsciousness again...

It isn't me that belongs in an institute; it is the sadists who found immense pleasure in my profound suffering. Lying down, I throw my face into my pillow, hoping to repress ghastly memories, but it doesn't work. My mind spits out more memories like a raging waterfall.

Even though I didn't want to give them the satisfaction of seeing me scared while I was asphyxiated, there was no hiding the truth. My lungs begged for oxygen. My eyes screamed for mercy that would never come. And my tears screamed about how my enemy was in charge, once again.

My only reprieve would be when the younger of my attackers were finally off to join Damien, who was already in college. This was an opportunity for me to embark on a journey called high school. Newfound space wasn't easily appreciated because it was so foreign to me. Without terror around every corner, I was almost at a loss. I had to convince myself to venture out of my norm and enjoy moments that were actually uninterrupted by trepidation. I had to start seeing hidden beauties, such as taking a shower without the fear of it being brutally invaded. During the week, when all the brothers were away, I started to allow my footfalls to actually make noise. To find my sanity again, I had to stop searching the shadows for danger.

I had to take a chance...

Standing on the sidewalk, getting ready to catch my school bus and head home, I was fifteen and a freshman. A teenager, happily running toward me, grabbed my full attention. He told me, "I couldn't help but notice how beautiful you are."

"Oh, God." I sit up in bed, hugging my pillow and curling over my lap, trying to find comfort that I'm starting to understand won't ever come.

Blue river eyes—

Chest seizing, my eyes race to my bedroom's window, desperate to see this young man in real life, but he's not here yet, and my memories now seem unstoppable.

Compared to what my life had been full of—beastly mistreatment—seeing this guy's raw innocence was like pumping pure sunshine into my veins. Unlike any young man I had known, he wasn't surrounded by sinister darkness. After the decrepit behavior I had been dealing with all my life, I couldn't help but smile in amazement. I had been ignored by all except my abusers. Now, here was this miracle. "Who are you?"

Precious dimples deepened. "Willing to find out?"

He was full of vitality, so unlike myself, and I inhaled his natural drug, immediately becoming addicted. "I think I am." I held out my hand. "I'm Lacey." I was nervous yet elated for my first friendship.

Beaming as if I were a dream come true for him, he accepted my hand for a shake. "I'm Tate." As we held hands, both not seeming to want to let go of the other, he added, "Isn't high school great?"

His hand felt like some sort of anchor to a whole new world. One where life wasn't irreversibly regrettable, but I eventually released his warmth. "I'm still getting adjusted, but yes. I think it will be awesome."

Studying me, he spoke in awe, "Your hair is even more beautiful up close."

The compliment had me peering down, bashfully, my fingers nervously tugging on the blonde strands hanging over my shoulder. I could barely utter, "Thank you."

He chuckled at my response. "Do you actually not know you're a pretty girl?"

A what? I gazed back up at him. A pretty girl? I, in all my years, never considered what I looked like to others. Due to my past, any mirror was an enemy. It showed only the sad reflection of a lost child that grew into a disturbed young woman. So, I couldn't fight the grand smile that took over the face he was complimenting.

Faking falling back two steps, Tate grabbed his chest as if I was attempting to steal his heart. "Damn. And you just got prettier."

That caused me to laugh, which caused me to jolt in surprise. I hadn't done such a thing since before my father died. Covering my mouth, I could feel the blood draining from my face. I even felt faint.

Tate rushed forward and whispered, "You good?"

I blinked to clear my mind of horrid thoughts and made up an excuse. "I think I am, uh... just hungry."

"Hungry?" Tate chuckled with surprise. "A pretty girl that admits they eat?" His comment confused me, but he added, "Tell me you like milkshakes because I happen to believe sugar solves everything."

I had no idea what sugar could do for broken spirits, but Tate sure made it tempting to find out. Biting my bottom lip, I pondered how to answer. How weird would I sound if I admitted I'd never had one? My mom couldn't afford to take us out to eat nor stock our refrigerator with ice cream. So, I shrugged.

Tate wiggled his eyebrows. "Are you trying to be mysterious?"

His joking tendencies were both confusing and enchanting. It was quickly becoming clear that I lacked proper social skills to understand his humor, but his captivating smile set me at ease. "Will you surprise me with your favorite flavor?"

With the brothers gone and Mom at work, I was free for this adventure. Driving in a little beat-up blue four-door car, I sat in the passenger seat, dumbfounded by how loud it was. Either Tate's muffler was faulty or didn't exist at all.

In anxious hands, I held a "surprise" milkshake that I wasn't allowed to taste yet. Tate swore it was better after melting for a few moments.

Tate turned his steering wheel and spoke, but I couldn't hear him over his car's roar, so I yelled, "What?"

He took a deep breath, then shouted, "How'd you get that scar?"

His eyes were studying the left side of my neck. I quickly covered it with my hair and yelled, "Accident."

Tate nodded them mouthed something.

"Huh?" I pointed to my ear then giggled.

Fighting laughter, Tate hollered, "I said, have you ever been to Loli Park?"

I hadn't, but that's not what had me laughing for the second time in years. "I think you just damaged your vocal cords!"

Now, he was laughing, too. I couldn't hear the laughter, of course, but I could see it. He playfully screamed, "Are you raggin' on my wheels?"

"The wheels aren't what's so noisy!" I held my belly through free laughter.

Whatever I said, for some reason, he found it hysterical, which became contagious to the point we both laughed all the way to the abandoned park.

The rusty swings and slides were a symbol of what I once wished to be; discarded and left alone. But now, after meeting Tate, happily subdued through laughter, I wondered what else I had been missing.

Sitting on the ancient merry-go-round, I folded my legs to get comfortable. Sitting beside me, Tate used his feet to propel us slowly in circles. Metal on metal squeaked as he told me, "Okay. Now you may try to guess the flavor."

I took a timid draw on my straw... then smiled at the wonderful taste. Blended banana and vanilla ice cream slid down my throat. "Oh my gosh. This is so good." I quickly took another sip.

Proudly, Tate gave me the most charming, genuine smile with an adorable light-hearted shrug. "See? Tate is wise." Then he sucked down some of his milkshake.

As if we had been best friends all our lives, we talked and talked. By the time we were done with the milkshakes, I felt like a true teenager—or, at least, what I had imagined a teenager to be like. That's why, when my long sleeve slipped up my arm, my heart plummeted. I didn't want Tate to see my damaged limb.

Seeming as if lost in thought, Tate's head tilted after I re-covered my horrid S scar. Then, slowly, his eyes rose to study the scar on the side of my neck. I tried to cover that scar again, but he immediately grabbed my wrist and yanked up my sleeve to examine.

The newfound sunshine in my veins instantly melted into fire-filled fear that burned me from the inside out. Never having spoken of my battle wounds, I tried to yank away.

The beautiful glow in Tate's eyes evaporated all at once. His bottom eyelids began to tremble as if the nerves there had been set on fire. He growled, "How did you get these?"

"Wh-What?" I had never shown anyone or confessed to the scar. "I, uh, hurt myself."

"Oh yeah?" he snapped. "I bet every injury is on your left side because you're right-handed."

My mouth gaped open. I had never realized that the brothers purposely did that, so it was easier to explain my "self-inflicted" injuries. "Hey, how do you know they are all on the left—"

Tate suddenly leapt off the merry-go-round, leaving me to go in circles by myself. I rushed to my knees and kept turning to see him pacing and mumbling, "This is not happening."

"T-Tate?" I started to shake. The playful boy had morphed into an angry young man.

Ignoring me, he threw his cup in a rage. "How is this possible?" Leftover milkshake splattered from the force. "She wasn't real!"

As the merry-go-round came to a stop, I noticed Tate holding the right side of his neck. There was something monumental under that palm. I just knew it, so I slowly stood. I was torn between running away and trying to learn more.

When Tate finally faced me, then stumbled forward, I knew my chance to run had ended. I knew I was no longer spinning from the merry-go-round. Now, life was taking me for a ride. His hand dropped from his neck to expose a thin scar, just like mine.

In front of me, Tate dropped to his knees. The pain, the hurt on his beautiful face, which no longer beamed with dimples, was shredding my heart. Everything about him screamed how defeated he felt. "I didn't know you were real."

Dread built in my gut and throat. We both knew there was an ugly truth, even before seeing all the evidence.

Staring up at me, Tate slowly lifted the long sleeve on his right arm to expose the corrupted slight swirl I knew all too well: the signature mark of my attackers.

A thunderstorm erupted in my lonely chest as I reached out to touch the raised skin that would never be the same again. I had to know it was real and that Tate wasn't some imaginary friend my subconscious had invented. We never lost eye contact—the soul to soul connection—as my fingertips grazed the branding.

Tate sounded broken as he told me, "I'm so sorry I never came for you."

How can such simple words have so much meaning? Because it meant someone else knew me. Someone, like my father, would have tried to help me.

My legs crumbled. Tate may not have succeeded, as my father didn't, but if he had...

Gasping for air, I found myself on my knees, face to face with Tate. My panting chest kept bumping into his. My breasts soft. His hard. Opposites, colliding and joining.

Was it divine intervention or simply coincidence? I don't know, but for the first time in my whole tortured existence, I wasn't alone.

There was Tate.
Damaged. Just like me.
I could see it in his exposed heart.

My eyes welled for the ill-treatment that I was sure he had experienced, and because I now had a comrade. As sad as that was, I was thankful to no longer be alone in the madness.

With such sorrow and surrender, Tate raised his right hand. On his palm was an *oval burn mark. "I'm left-handed."*

I found myself raising my left, so many notions falling into place. "From a spoon."
Our painful pasts and futures lingered in the air between us.

Pity, sympathy, and complete understanding crossed his face as he nodded. "They boiled it in a pot first."

My stomach churned at the memory. "It felt like fire."

His whisper was weighted down by a sadness only the two of us would ever understand. "For days."

Even though we were speaking of a horrid time, our hands stayed facing each other as if silently speaking to the broken spirits who they belonged to.

A tear slipped down my cheek. "Yes, for days." Drifting forward, my hand touched Tate's.

As if completely lost of all hope, Tate's forehead drifted down to mine. "You're real."

My fingers closed around his as I softly asked, "How do you know me?"

Still connected, physically and emotionally, he replied, "When I was a little boy, I had a best friend. Her name was Lucy. At least, that's what I called her. The brothers never stopped me." I was surprised he referred to my abusers in the same manner. It was as if their names brought too much reality to this situation we both hoped didn't truly exist. Tate continued. "She held my heart in the palm of her hand. But, after one night, I never saw her again. I thought—I thought I had dreamt her up." He took a few deep breaths. "The brothers put my tiny Lucy in a small duffle bag—"

In my bedroom, sitting on my bed, I instantly think of the memory I spoke to Doctor Landon about... *"The bag I'm in makes a* swish *sound as it's dragged across hard flooring. It's drowning out the crying..."* It was Tate who had been crying.

Tate's breath smelled like vanilla as he whispered, "I cried so long and hard for that little girl who was thrown down the stairs. My brothers left me home after that. I never saw you again. I'm so sorry. I eventually believed I had made you up in my mind."

Comprehending his desperation on the deepest of level, I moved my cheek so it could lay against his. I needed this affection as much as I wanted to give it. Even though I didn't remember him yet, I sensed the unity we two little children had. We had already been fighting beasts before ever hearing of scary fairytales.

A body close to mine, one that meant me no harm, was like touching an angel. Slowly, as if not believing this miracle to be true, I released his hand and raised my arms to hold him.

Tate responded by melting into me. His arms wrapped around my waist, as hungry as I for kindness. "Does it make me an asshole to say I'm glad you're real?"

"Only if it makes me one." I had wanted another destroyed soul to be with me through every act of violence. I wanted someone by my side while my life was gutted. But, now knowing Tate had suffered, I felt I had been selfish to ever wish for him at all.

I should have wanted professional assistance—Police or someone to stop the vicious crimes, but when you are lost in traumatic cycles, common sense can be far from your reasoning. Escaping had never been a hope for me. All hope was consumed with the need to survive each episode.

It's like your world and the real world never meet. Not truly. My abuse had me feeling isolated, like an alien lost on earth. I felt I didn't belong. I felt I was walking a planet and seeing it from eyes no one else had. Therefore, no human would understand what I was hiding.

Only Tate.

Again, I look to my bedroom window, hoping to see Tate crawling through. But only the moon is present, so I slip into another memory to have him close.

Leaving Tate's car parked in the street, we stood staring at the outside of my dilapidated two-story home. Tate was dumbfounded. "I've been past this house a million times. I live two blocks over. Had I only known who was inside."

Standing next to him, I stated, "No one knows who's inside."

A warm hand slipped inside mine. "I do now."

I gazed at my abused hero who could never save me. "I'm glad."

Was it surprising we didn't speak of rescuing each other? Maybe. I'm not sure. I've never—we never—had a life without severe abuse. I'm not sure what the proper reaction should have been. Maybe the abused don't have "proper" reactions. Maybe enduring is enough.

Walking through the front door, Tate gawked at the staircase as if it were deadly. From the top, his stare traveled down until reaching the floor under his feet. "This is

where you landed." His eyes closed with a grimace. "Your little cry... It was so helpless."
His head fell forward. "So was I. I'm sorry."

That fall had caused a headache that lasted for a long time. Now, I'm understanding I had an actual head injury. My mother had given me a child's pain reliever with no professional care, not knowing I was in need. Maybe that is why I have amnesia now. Either way... "I remember you now, Tate."

In my room, Tate studied my carpet. "No stains. I have one." Then he observed my bathroom. I didn't bother to mention my bed had been moved over the prior stain. After a labored exhale, he nodded. "They learn quickly." As he walked around my room again, I studied how male he was. His feet, his hands, thick thighs... All equaling strength.

I sat on the edge of my bed. "How do they overpower you?"

Tate observed as if reading my mind; he was considerably stronger than me. He ran stressed fingers through his shaggy hair. "My mom." Before he finished with, "I'll do anything for her," I was already nodding in complete agreement.

"Your dad?"

He ran a hand down his exasperated face then spoke as if a programmed robot. "Drowned. Freak accident."

My stomach twisted. "You mean they killed him."

With an incredible amount of awareness, Tate's eyes snapped to mine.

My chest ached as I nodded. Trying not to experience the loss all over again, I gazed at my dad's picture on my dresser. "My dad... had an 'accidental' fall."

With fear-laced blue eyes that I wished never had to know tragedy, Tate stood there motionless for a while, then those eyes watered. His voice cracked, probably mimicking his already broken heart. "Have I made you up?"

Seeing his evident pain, my throat tightened. "No."

As if needing more proof, Tate sat next to me, his palm cupping my cheek. So he could trust his senses, I leaned into his touch, appreciating his burn scar because it made me feel closer to him. "I've been alone for so long."

Losing my breath from pity and my own aching loneliness, I nodded, empathetically, and kissed his palm before nuzzling into it again. "Me too."

After a moment, he decided to confess more than his father's murder. "I tried to tell a teacher once." I gasped at the young man braver than I. "I was young. All this was hard to articulate, so she didn't believe me."

My shaky hand reached up to touch his innocent face that had seen too much in his short life. *"I'm sorry."* I exhaled disappointment. *"I never tried. I was there when..."* I whispered as if the brothers could hear me, *"they killed him."* Tate swallowed while staring at me as if sensing how trapped we believed we were. *"Even if I got someone to believe me... Who would protect my mom? They hate me so much—"*

"They would be sure to kill her as revenge, no matter what it took—"

"They would punish me."

Now, Tate kissed my palm. He inhaled against my skin as if wanting to capture me in his lungs. *"Through all this hell, I have found me the perfect angel."*

Now knowing more through Doctor Landon, I can see some of the mistakes Tate and I made. We let fear control us. That terror of the unknown crippled us. If you don't believe you have legs, how can you run? If you are blind to freedom, it will never be yours.

"Lacey? Do my brothers..." His hand reached out and gently touched my hip. *"Do they..."* He swallowed. *"I'm a guy, so they don't... you know, but... you're a girl. Do they... do more than 'hurt' you?"*

Even though the rapes weren't my fault, Tate not experiencing the same abuse somehow made me more shameful about the horrendous acts. I wondered what he would have thought about the incest. I was fearful he would think less of me. Since my opinion of myself was critically beneath healthy standards, the only best friend I had ever had, no matter how many years ago, thinking I was disgusting was like a death sentence. Tate coming back into my life, even though I barely knew him, was a surge of hope. One I needed most desperately.

I already lacked the ability to lie to Tate, but I also lacked the will to tell him the truth. So, I only stared at him, not offering fuel for his growing suspicion.

Tate's eyes closed in remorse. He spoke with a truth I could feel in my bones. *"I'm so sorry I ever wished you to life."*

"All the wishes in the world can't change what is already done."

"I want to change what happens next."

"We both know the risk isn't worth it. My only option is—" I eyed him, wondering if I dared to speak my true thoughts.

Absolute sorrow laced his voice. "Maybe, with each other, we will want to live."

And there it was. The truth. Our lives were so horrid we struggled to want to live. It was hopeless.

Tate's scarred hand left my cheek and grabbed mine. Our fingers interlocked with a haunting desperation. Then we stared at each other, forming a silent bond that wouldn't end.

"Lacey, I won't give up until you do."

I burst into tears while forcing a smile. "That's a lot of pressure for a girl."

He shook our connected hands and teased, "A pretty girl."

Shakily, I exhaled the fear building inside me. He was asking for me to keep fighting. "Yes, a pretty girl."

Tate's free hand caressed my cheek. His thumb grazed my lips before he told me, "I've never kissed anyone before."

I stared at his mouth, wanting a taste. "Neither have I."

Saddened, he softly asked, "How could they use you yet never want a kiss?"

I told him the truth. "They prefer this mouth to scream."

Tate's mouth opened, but his appall was only slight. He had experienced plenty to know what I was referring to. His own torture had taught him well.

Deep inside me, a surrender took place, knowing I was no longer alone. Tears dripped down my face. "I would love to be your first."

As if knowing this would become our only solace, Tate's eyes watered as his lips gently touched mine. A soft sob escaped us both with a beautiful moment like we had never known. The tenderness, the kindness, and the friendship had us silently praying for more stolen moments. With how our lives were, we never knew when the next one would be.

I sniffled, then forced a sad smile. "You taste like vanilla."

"See?" Tate's fake smile caused his tears to finally fall. "Sugar fixes everything."

Soft lips touched mine again...

Wiping tears for the lost souls, I look to the window and whisper, "Tate, where are you?"

CHAPTER FIVE

Memories to Life

I wish to run from the hurt, but my feet can't find the ground
Without the earth... I will never be found.

There wasn't enough sugar in the world to keep the brothers from finding out about the growing love affair... I whisper a prayer, "Please, let there be a merciful God."

So tired from all this emotional upheaval, my swollen eyes want to shut, but my mind has been pried open and now demands on continuing the beautiful and painful journey of my poisonous past. Watching the empty window as if a sailor's wife waiting to see a ship float into a harbor, I lie down on my side, hoping the pillow can carry me until Tate comes.

With the brothers preoccupied with college, Tate and I had a suspended-in-the-clouds romance. Our connection effortlessly grew. There was an unseen link that could be felt between lifetimes. I was sure of it.

HOSTILE ILLUSIONS

Wounded souls and hearts with holes
May you forever be
Lovers of the night, willing to fight
May you forever... be

Tate and I let our battle scars lead us to a peaceful place no abuser could reach. Every caress of his lips belonged to only me. Every embrace and kind word I offered him, no one else heard that from me. We were peace and grace while being set on fire.

Fire...

Late one night, my mother was still at work when all four brothers came home for an unscheduled visit. In my darkened room, I quickly laid in my bed and covered myself, hoping they would think I was asleep, and that they would give a damn.

They didn't do either.

Some women may have celebrated their menstrual cycle, as they should since it means life—a chance for reproduction—but I loathed the bloody week and the criminal acts it brought me. The brothers were ruthless...

In my dark bedroom, I laid on my side in the fetal position, crying. I didn't fear being overheard because the brothers had left in a car once they were done with me. I watched my window open, and Tate crawled through.

I reached out my scarred hand.

Grabbing my hand, he rushed to kneel next to my bed. "I didn't know they had come home. How bad?"

Tears dripped... "It hurts. So deep."

Tate's face reddened as he tried to control his fury. "Do you need a hospital?"

That was never an option for us, but I appreciated him willing to risk his mother's life for me. I did need a hospital. The damage done to my womb would cause permanent damage. "No, I will be fine."

He looked to my nightstand and grimaced before laying his forehead to my hand. "Lacey, let me take you to the hospital."

"Please, throw them away."

Tate's body seemed to tremble as he stood and grabbed the enormous cucumber and other objects I had just been violated with. "I will get you those antibiotics."

We both stole every leftover drug that had been subscribed to our moms or brothers for any ailment—

I try to remember ever being taken to a doctor by my mom. I wince in pain as I start to understand the twins were my mother's favorite, to a gross degree. I can't say whether or not she knew of the abuse, but I can say she was a very absent parental figure.

Tate returned from the bathroom with a cup of water and two pills in his palm. He set the medication bottle on the nightstand. "You know the drill. Finish that bottle. Okay?"

I accepted and swallowed my only chance of avoiding an infection. "Will it ever end?"

Urgently, and with anguish in his eyes, he made his way around my small bed to crawl in behind me. Holding me tight, he burrowed against my neck with a heavy whisper, "It will. I swear it. Someday."

Maybe Tate's promises were gold because my attacks did stop. Tate's didn't, which was peculiar...

"Oh no... No, no, no, no." I rush from the bed at Serenity and to the window. My hands lay on the cool glass, silently begging for river eyes to appear.

When Tate missed two days of school, after the brothers visited home, I went to his house in the middle of the night and knocked on his window. From his bed, Tate opened his eyes and smiled, bringing me immense relief. I snuck in, whispering, "You scared me."

"Someone needin' some sugar?"

Trying to muffle my giggle, I quickly crawled into his bed. I stopped when he winced. "What's wrong?"

With effort, he laid an arm out for me to come to his side. "Cracked ribs was the flavor of this trip." When I didn't move, his smile faded. "You are the only healing that will make this better. Lay with me."

Tears rushed from my eyes as I carefully snuggled to his bruised side. "Tate, why didn't they hurt me this time?"

He kissed the top of my head after a deep inhale of my hair. His arm curled around me, even though I was sure it was causing him more pain. "Don't ask me to question a blessing, Pretty Girl."

My tears dripped to his damaged chest. "Okay, Tate."

"Don't leave me until I fall asleep."

I tried to swallow an audible sob, but it was like swallowing my heart whole. Impossible since my heart thundered for the most precious being in my world. "Okay, Tate."

His tired whisper was pure honesty. "I love you, Lacey."

The cool glass no longer offers comfort against my heated skin. "Tate, I need you to come to me." My eyes dare to open, but I wish I'd never opened them. For the first time since being at Serenity, I finally see iron bars at my window. "No." I slide up the window and touch the cold bars that are screaming a reality I don't want to see. *"No."* I grab them and try to rattle the obstruction that was not here before, but they are solid and unforgiving to my soul.

Nor were more memories attacking me.

Now a sophomore in high school, Tate was in excruciating pain. The brothers had just left for college, and Tate had made his way to me. Standing in my bathroom, he peered down at me on my knees in front of him. "I'm not pulling down my pants, Pretty Girl."

"Let me see!" I grinned. "I won't judge your shortcomings." Again, I reached for his buckle only to be shooed away.

"Shortcomings?" He laughed while faking being appalled. "If my balls weren't sliced, I'd tell you—"

I smacked his thigh. "Pants. Down. Now."

After an exhale that told me I'd won, Tate finally unbuckled his jeans and pulled them down along with his boxers.

His penis was flaccid but still held my attention. I tried to curve my curiosity and focus on his wound. "Can you lift it so I can see?"

Tate teased, "See? Not short. You're not even sure it's possible to lift this beast."

It was nothing if not amazing that he and I could find it possible to joke around when, in truth, we were experiencing another result from crude humans conflicting lesions on another.

Tate lifted his penis to expose his testicles. All jokes aside, the action had him throwing his head back and knocking it into my bathroom wall.

I hissed at the sight. "Oh, Tate. I'm sorry." I quickly turned to the cabinets behind me and grabbed some ointment. When I faced him again, I apologized before attempting to spread some on his sensitive area.

Understandably, Tate jerked away. "Fuck! It hurts so bad, Lace!"

I swallowed down sorrow because his pain was my pain. His hurt was my hurt. It was as if I felt everything he did because I adored him that much. "Okay. I won't touch you there."

I moved his hand from his penis, which had him asking, "What are you—" Tate gasped as I took his soft length in my mouth. "Lace—" His head hit the wall again, but this time, it was in pleasure. Tate grew in my mouth, telling me he was no longer focused on his cruel injury. While my mouth worked him, my lubricated fingers slowly found their way to the laceration and dabbed ointment...

Still gripping the bars, a breeze in the night blows across my face, giving me the fresh air needed to recover from his pain. I stare into the woods Tate had rushed from to visit me in the garden. Tears run down my face as I realize it may have all been another illusion.

Tate's mom was now spending all extra minutes with her new boyfriend. She was spending nights with him, too. I didn't judge her for clinging to a man. I was doing the same.

In his bedroom, Tate's tongue delved into my mouth as his body rocked on top of me. After two more years, we were no longer inexperienced lovers. We knew how to gift each other highs that we could ride out into the night. My soft thighs clung to his strong hips that surged with an expertise that had me groaning with a fed hunger, yet I was glutton. "More, Tate," I moaned, already ravished yet begging.

Eager hands slipped under my shoulders, wrapped around, and gripped tight. I loved it when he did this. It was as if he was cementing me to this earth, in his arms, while joining his body with mine. As he pulled on me, his length pushed through my drenched channel until it was seated as deep as possible. Tate didn't retreat. He let us enjoy the sensation as I pulsed around him, on the verge of exploding into the most desired oblivion.

"I love you, Tate."

Gasping for air, since I had him enraptured, he chuckled, "Goddamnit," then grunted, "You know not to talk to me like that—" He ejaculated before finishing his sentence. I wrapped my legs around his butt, insisting he stayed planted inside me because it drove him wild. "Shiiiiiiiiit..."

His climax began to draw one from me. Even with all his weight on me, my body arched as my own high sensually ripped through me.

Knowing me on a level that was limitless, Tate started rocking his hips again to complete my mountain climb. I mewed at the sensation that took me into a private world. Stars raced through my mind, whether my eyes were opened or closed. Light storms danced through every molecule my body possessed. Then, boom, I orgasmed so hard it felt like a meteor fell from the sky and hit the earth with an immeasurable explosion.

Our sweat combined as we both laid in silence and awe. Our minds were free...

Sensing what is to come, I cover my mouth, begging myself not to vomit and alert an orderly to my distress.

Laughter boomed in Tate's living room, waking us.

Tate covered my mouth when he saw a scream building inside me. "Shh." Huddling over me, he shook as he stared at his closed bedroom door. "They're here for me. Not you." He suddenly leapt from his bed and forcefully yanked me to my feet, then dragged me to his closet. Lips slammed to mine. "You don't come out for nothing. You understand me?" Then he shoved me into his closet before closing the door. "Don't watch, Lace."

Absolutely horrified, I stood, naked and motionless, as Tate's bedroom door swung open. "Where are you, fucker?"

Tate backed away from me as if leading the predator away. "I'm here." He faced the evil ones. "Now, get the fuck out."

Jarod laughed. "Oh, good. He's ready to play."

As Tate grabbed jeans from a chair and tugged them on, I saw four dark figures enter his unlit room and prowl toward him. "Fuck all four of you." Tate kept backing away, drawing the attention away from where I hid.

Falling to my knees, I puke on the floor.

This is why I had been spared so often by the brothers. Tate had been taunting them, daring their attack, so they were too tired to come after me.

I wipe my mouth as the memory continues...

While loud arguing took place, I quietly pulled a sweatshirt from a hanger and slipped it on. I grabbed a pair of Tate's sweatpants from the ground and pulled them on, tightening the drawstring to hold them up.

Suddenly, the brothers were wrestling with Tate, forcing him into his bathroom, dragging a chair with them. Soon, he was screaming. His pain is my pain... *I ran from the closet, yelling, "Stop it!" and rushed to the bathroom to see the gruesome act of the brothers removing one of Tate's molars.*

They stopped. Five sets of eyes found me. One set sadder than I had ever seen. The other four sets, more livid than ever before.

Jarod started to shake in a madness I couldn't comprehend. "What are you doing here?" He didn't even give me a chance to answer before looking back to Tate in the chair, blood dripping from his lips. "Have you been fucking my sister?" Jarod spoke as if disrespected. He spoke as if he weren't fucking me himself.

Tate kept spitting up blood, unable to reply.

His desperate state had me shoving past the stunned brothers and grabbing a rag. With compassion, I told Tate, "Open your mouth."

River blue eyes bored into mine as he obliged me. He tried to talk, "Should've stayed."

Placing the corner of the cloth in his mouth, I cried, "Evermore." Tate's shoulders shook as he began to break down, sensing the horror my actions would cause. I kissed his bloody mouth, "Evermo—" then was yanked away by my hair.

On my knees, I grab at the left side of my face. I can remember Tate's agonized screams around the rag in his mouth as he was held back while my own molar was torn from my mouth. I must've passed out because I have no recollection until waking in the trunk of my brother's car.

Tate was with me, running fingers through my hair as my eyes fluttered open. His fingers didn't have much to touch. My hair had been hacked off as if the brothers were enraged at me. Tate still had blood around his lips that was cracked, as if drying long ago. I tried to move but quickly realized Tate and I were compacted in the small confinement. Only light from the taillights lit the trunk.

On his side, facing me, he tried to talk around his swollen cheek. "You've been out for a whole day."

He helped me pull a rag from my mouth. "W—" I winced then held my sore cheek.

"Where are we?"

Tate appeared to be in a surrendered calm as if he had given up. "I don't know. They have been driving us for hours."

It was easy to imagine why the brothers were driving us far from home. "They are going to kill us, aren't they?"

His nod was solemn and tired. "Yeah."

Even though it hurt, I bit on my lips, so scared and sad. Tears leaked from my eyes that burned from exhaustion and dehydration. "I should have stayed in the closet."

Tate's swollen lips trembled as he attempted a smile. "No. You were so brave; it made me love you even more."

My heart split wide open, and I sobbed. "I will miss you so much, Tate."

"Shh." Barely any room, Tate still leaned his head forward to mine. "No. We will be together. Lacey, say it. No matter what, we will find each other."

Trying to catch my breath, I wiped his tears. "N-No matter what. E-Evermore."

Crusty, quivering, yet beautiful lips touched mine. "Evermore."

Soon, we were bouncing in the trunk as if headed down an old dirt road. Once the car stopped, my heart pounded. This was it. And, if the brothers were epically cruel when composed, with how mad they were, this death was going to be horrendous.

The trunk opened. Tate did his best to hold on to my hands, but four on one was too much. Overpowered, he screamed for me to run, but I didn't even have a chance to climb out of the trunk before one of his brothers had me in their grasp.

My wrists were being bound together by a thick rope as a Jake told Tate, "Don't worry. You can have her again." The opposite end of the rope was placed in the trunk before it was slammed shut. "As soon as you catch her."

I stood there, dumbfounded to his meaning until they all loaded back into the car and started the motor. Tate's eyes raced from my wrist to the trunk. All blood rushed from his face. "Oh, Jesus, no." But there was nothing to be done.

The car went into drive... Then dragged me down the dirt road...

Tate's sweatpants or sweatshirt, nor his screams of rage, could save me. My little body took a beating. Tate ran as fast as he could to catch up to me, but the car was too quick.

Mercifully, my head finally hit a rock, and I was knocked unconscious.

In the fetal position, I open my eyes. "Tate." I pull my traumatized body from the ground and back to the window with bars. "T-Tate." I inhale, hoping to smell his manly scent. "I... need you."

Coughing is what woke me.

In so much pain, lying on my back, my head lobbed to the left to see Tate, also on his back. His right hand shook while reaching out to me. There was an immense amount of blood all over his sternum as if he had been savagely stabbed, over and over.

To help him touch me, my left hand moved slightly. My voice cracked. "I'm here."

The brothers were gone. I can only presume they took us for dead or dying.

Shell-shocked river eyes shot to mine. "Lace—" Blood spurted from his mouth.

A sob ripped from my shattered body and heart as I gripped his fingers. "I'm here. I'm here, Tate."

Tate had never cried so hard in front of me before, but maybe that's what happens when you're saying goodbye. There is nothing left to hide, so you do and say what needs to be. "You find me, okay?"

My body jolted through every heartbreaking howl that escaped me. "Okay, Tate. I will. I promise."

Blood leaked from his mouth. "Evermore."

Our scarred palms touched one another tight until... Tate's went still.

If I were to have combined every torture the brothers inflicted on me, all at once, it wouldn't even begin to compare to the pain of losing Tate. I'm sure my screams were heard for miles... until they finally died, too.

Left without an ounce of hope, I stared into Tate's dead eyes, and envied his death.

My returned memory is like witnessing the love of my life dying all over again. Anguished keening sneaks out from somewhere deep within my body as acid eats away at my heart. Breathing in air is like inhaling razor blades... I simply can't live like this!

They weren't illusions at all.
They were memories.
Maybe that is the case for all of us.
We're not mad. We're simply... destroyed.

Knowing Tate is never coming to me again, I slam the window shut so hard I want the devil himself to wake. I want him to suffer! But the hospital stays quiet. Only a crack in the glass is heard.

The broken glass is a symbol of me, so I use it to search for my Tate. I take the shard and slice my wrist and beg myself to return to the woods the night Tate perished—the night I made a promise I have every intention on keeping.

When my legs weaken, I let them carry me back to the floor so I can rest.

As I lie here, life draining from my body, there is a clarity that is bringing me a cherished peace. I smile in relief, knowing that there is truly an Evermore, as I sense him waiting for me.

The trees before me bow and bend to the wind that rushes through. A few leaves surrender to the grand force and fall from where they once belonged. I watch them float downward... as if dancing in celebration for my choice.

I exhale... *Choice. It is finally mine.*

"You should've waited for my sugar."

My last exhale is with serenity. "Tate."

I found him.

EPILOGUE

What was it like to find Lace lying on her hospital room floor, bleeding out? It was a massacre of the heart. Running past her bed, I dropped to my knees and slid to her side. The VP I had hoped would patch me in some day, followed me, immediately putting pressure on her wrist—the one above the scar on her left palm.

Her left... This time, is was actually her who caused harm to her perfect skin.

"Lace," I whispered through a sob.

I had just made love to her the night before when I realized she was finally remembering me. The time had finally come. I knew it was time to bring her back to my new home—our new home. We couldn't chance moving a mentally shattered girl before then. What she had been through... I didn't dare push her before she was ready.

When I returned that night, the bars on her room that I had taken off so I could hold her, had been replaced. Not having proper tools, we chose breaking-and-entering as a last resort. It was easy. The building was old and so were the locks.

Sneaking up the stairs with everyone sleeping, except one orderly making his rounds, made me think we were home free. Now I was staring at a pale version of the girl I was here to rescue from a life that almost killed us.

VP was checking her pulse as I touched her angelic face. I hissed when my hand left a trail of her own blood. "No." My eyes followed the blood... A piece of glass in her right hand.

Right hand...

Fighting shock and the knowledge that living without Lace wasn't an option, I held up my right hand to stare at her blood... and my own scar in the center of my palm. Then, my eyes went back to the piece of glass. I reached out for it...

A grip on my shoulder shook me. A deep whisper sounded, "Not happenin'."

Peering up, I saw my Prez. The door was shut behind him. Even in the dark room, he took up all the space around me. Yes, he was a large man, but it was what he had become to me in the last two months that was larger than the life I now wanted to leave behind.

Tightening the hold on my shoulder, he lifted his chin. "We never give up. Hear me?"

Dazed, my eyes found Lace again. "But, my... pretty girl." I've heard guys say 'she's my everything' but they had never had a Lacey. If they did, they would know *she* is everything.

"Kid," my VP whispered, not letting up on stopping her blood flow. "Look at me."

It felt like asking the sun not to shine when he asked me not to keep staring at the beautiful girl who owned my fucking soul. But, for once, I had men I could turn to.

They had found me in the woods one night, claiming to have followed the most pitiful female screams they had ever heard. *Lace...*

It was the night my brothers stabbed me, leaving me for dead.

That night was the beginning of a goodbye to blood brothers and a hello to brothers that would never fail me.

Never. Especially this night.

A foreign sensation in my gut and chest burned as I watched my Prez rip his T-shirt into strips.

"That's it, kid." My VP lifted Lacey's hand so my Prez could wrap her wrist tight with the material. "We fight until there ain't nothin' left to fight for."

Prez tied a knot that made me think of how Lace and I will always be intertwined.

Then he checked the little window in the door. "We're clear." Turning the knob, he told me, "Pick up your girl. Let's get 'er home."

Home... A safe place.

I cried. I shook. But I got off my knees and picked up my Lace—my *evermore.*

R. ADAMS

Oh, this story and what it has done to my heart! I hope you have enjoyed Lacey and Tate as much as I have. They are beautiful souls, lost in a life that was far too cruel.

So many readers have reached out to me, wanting Lacey and Tate to have their day.

Well, it is coming... Preorder *Hostile Vengeance*, the first novel in the Steel Stallions MC series, that releases April 8th 2021

Until that release, you can also see more of Lace and Tate in Bleed Me, the third interconnected-standalone in the Haunted Roads series.

And, if you need to holler at me because I made you cry, my reader group will totally have your back. This is where they attempt to keep me in line: Facebook group, India R. Adams' Flames. You can also get another FREE India novella, *Blue Waters*, by signing up for my newsletter!

Burn bright and beautiful,

India

THANK YOUS

Thank you to Cat for being by my side, every single step of this crazy journey! You, as always, go so far and beyond being my PA. You are my friend. You're a soul sister. And a cover and formatting goddess.

Thank you to Deb for being gracious, uplifting, completely supportive, and for being a fantastic Alpha reader.

Thank you to Kendra for saving my ass! If every author had an editor with such heart, they would all be as happy as me. Once you have worked on my manuscripts, I always feel relief that my book will be the best it can be for my readers.

Thank you to ARC readers and Reviewers. You are amazing and always getting this India train rolling on social media and all over the internet!

And, a special thank you to my readers who, no matter what, have my back, heart, and soul.

As always, without my family's support, Author India would not exist!

ABOUT THE AUTHOR

India R Adams is an author/singer/songwriter who has written YA and NA novels such as *My Wolf and Me*, *Blue Waters* (A Tainted Water Novella), *Steal Me* (A Haunted Roads Novel), *Rain* (A Stranger in the Woods Novel), and *Serenity* (A Forever Novel), as well as music for the *Forever* series.

India was born and raised in Florida but has also been lucky enough to live in Idaho (where she froze but fell in love with the small-town life), Austin, Texas (where she started her first book, *Serenity* and met wonderful artists), and now Murphy, North Carolina (where the mountains have stolen a piece of her heart).

Being a survivor of abuse has inspired India to let others know they have nothing to be ashamed of. She has used her many years of professional theater experience to build characters and stories with dark undercurrents that stem from her personal life. She says, "I'm simply finding ways to empower perfect imperfections."

Another thing India feels needs much more awareness is sexual slavery. She has joined forces with jewelers to design beautiful ways to raise money for nonprofit organizations. Even though India writes about serious subjects such as domestic violence, sexual abuse, and human trafficking, she has a magnificent sense of humor, as do the characters she creates. Her novels are perfectly balanced between laughter and tears, letting readers see how to empower their *own* perfect imperfections.

CONNECT WITH INDIA

Want to get in touch with India? She loves hearing her readers thoughts!
You can email her : india@indias.productions
Or join her reader group on Facebook : India R. Adams' Flames
Check out her website for updates on all things India!
http://indias.productions
If you want to stay in the loop, make sure you sign up to her newsletter!

BOOKS BY INDIA

Tainted Water
Blue Waters
Black Waters
Red Waters
Volatile Waters
Ashen Waters (Coming Winter 2020)

Ivy's Poison

Haunted Roads
Steal Me
Scar Me
Bleed Me

A Stranger in the Woods
Rain
River
Mist
The Travelers (Coming June 11th 2021) (Standalone)
My Wolf and Me (Standalone)

Forever
Serenity
Destiny
Mercy
Hope (Coming Fall 2020)

Redemption Ryders MC
Road to Redemption (Coming 2021)

Steel Stallions MC
Hostile Illusions (Prequel)
Hostile Vengeance (Coming April 8th 2021)

PLAYLIST

Spotlight artists:
Freya Ridings, thank you for being so deep and dark, giving me much
inspiration!
Alterbridge, thank you for you album, Walk the Sky.
"One Life" by Alterbridge
""Wouldn't You Rather" by Alterbridge
"You Were Good To Me" by Keremy Zucker & Chelsea Cutler
"Poison" by Frey Ridings
"In the Deep" Alterbridge
"Ultraviolet" by Freya Ridings
"Silent All These Years" by Tori Amos
"Fully Alive" by Flyleaf
"Fine Again" by Seether
"Love in the Dark" by Jessie Reyez
"Blackout" by Freya Ridings
"The After You" by Miakoda

Made in United States
Troutdale, OR
12/22/2024

27174191R00048